FIDELITIES

a chronology

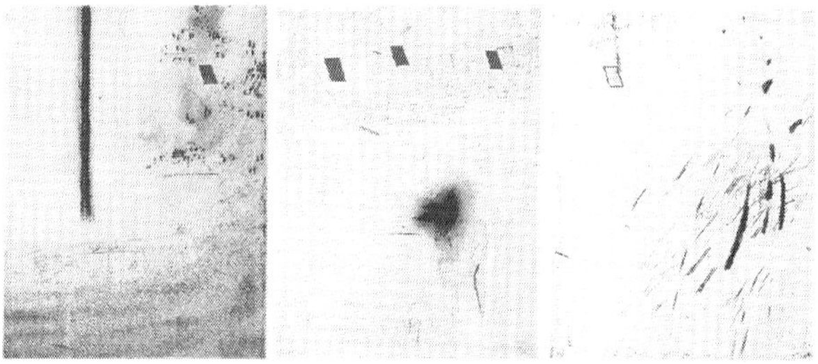

KEITH TAYLOR

Alice Greene & Co. Ann Arbor, Michigan

Alice Greene & Co.
P.O. Box 7406
Ann Arbor, MI 48107
www.alicegreene.com

ISBN 978-1-935770-14-5

Illustration: "Earthbound III" by Takeshi Takahara
Book Design: Jean Buescher Bartlett
Cover Design: Gail Dennis
Assistance: Colin O'Brien

Printed in the United States of America

for Christine

I might stand on a catwalk
built through a forest canopy
with any stranger. I could stare
into the eye of a cerulean warbler
frantically singing to mark territory
or call in a mate. But if I walk
through a vineyard that slopes
down toward the sea, I will
walk, my love, only with you.

We must have
the stubborness to accept our gladness in the ruthless
furnace of this world.

–*Jack Gilbert,* "A Brief for the Defense"

DRUMMOND ISLAND FOSSILS

Take the ferry east out of Detour
then drive up across the alvar plains
to a path that leads you to the shore.
There, rock ledges step down to the lake.
Kneel. Look closely. You'll see shadows, then
limestone honey-combed with delicate
coral branches that waved from the floor
of an ocean we can't imagine.

STONE TOOLS

after John M. O'Shea

Three thousand years ago someone stopped
on a small hill, unnoticed now
behind a post-war subdivision
but only a block up from the river.

He sat on a large rock, a glacial
erratic, for an afternoon and chipped
a stone point from a piece of chert.

He left his sharp-edged flakes scattered
and glistening under the oak leaves.

AEGINA: AFTER SCHOOL

She was six or seven and was the last child off the bus. She kicked her way through the pines and across the cracked marble.

We paid her father twenty-five drachmas for admission to the grounds. We had taken a boat out from Piraeus that morning, then caught a bus up the mountain to the Temple of Aphaia, a local goddess lost in forest or sea. We came for the pines and view and wind through the double colonnade. But we sat in the shade to watch the child – tiny, and ignoring the out of season tourists:

Black haired child kicking
        stones across the temple yard,
bored by the last
        three tourists in November.

STATUE OF THE BLIND GIRL

Nydia, the blind flower-girl of Pompeii
after Edward Bulwer-Lytton and Randolph Rogers

She listens, not to the green world exploding
around her, not to Vesuvius howling –

the hour has come; of two working in the field
one shall be taken; of two women grinding wheat
one shall be taken; Vesuvius erupts
and the black clouds descend; now we know
this is the hour when the thief will come –

she listens, not to the temples collapsing
or the birds crying from shriveled gardens,

she listens for the one voice who must call,
the one who knows, now that the hour has come,
that she can take us to the boats

and she suffers with our trembling earth,
gagging like the rest of us in this closed air,

but when we walk around her,
to the shadowed side, closer to the wall,
we can see the hidden profile,

the one that disguises her joy

now that the hour has come,
the one that shows her smile.

GIRL WITH A PEARL EARRING

Perhaps her nose
is more delicate,
or the woman you know

is older
and has never looked
over her shoulder

like that, cheeks flushed—
not at you
anyway. Still

she's familiar, someone
you might have had lunch with,
years ago.

SEA AND RAIN: LAKE MICHIGAN

after James McNeill Whistler

There is a dance at water's edge,
a movement between the lake, its sand
and the horizon where lake becomes cloud.

Between those lines our world's
a thin wash of muted tones, beige
and gray with a hint of white,

almost abstract, until the dancer
steps out into the pool.
She makes the whole thing real.

Grey stumps of white pines were almost charred into immortality by a fire so hot it burned off all the organic matter in the top several inches of soil. Little but lichen grew here for 130 years,

and now,
finally,
a clump of small,
ripe
blueberries.

PRAIRIE FIRE

i.m.: Donald Taylor

Uncertain about the difference
between his memory and the myth,
the thing he'd been told and what he'd seen,
he kept the image of rising clouds
of black smoke looming like dark mountains
to the west, with a flickering skirt
of fire growing larger, noisier,
dancing through the grass toward home.

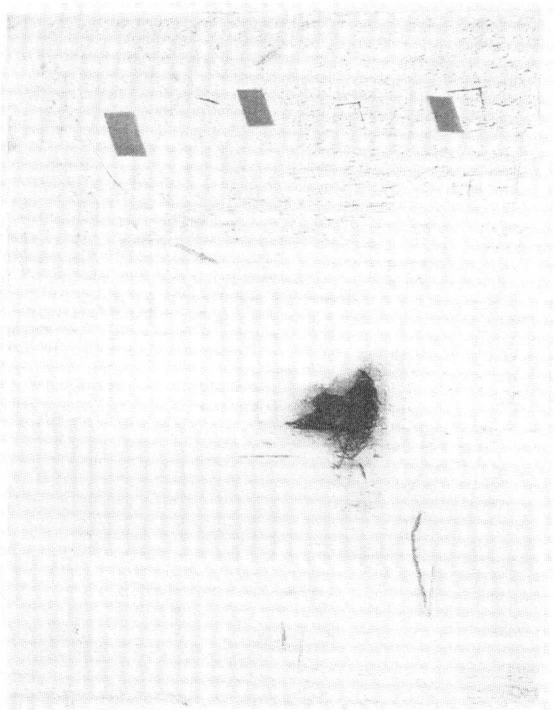

BANFF: RUNNING AWAY

I was young enough to believe that when moments felt significant they probably were. I saw sacraments everywhere

so knee deep in snow
behind the picnic shelter
where I went to take a leak
I looked up
at mountains only
partially cloud shrouded

and was sure that this must mean something. But metaphor wasn't imminent, or it was hiding just past the edge of my loneliness.

It was the thing to do, so a few months before my sixteenth birthday I volunteered to work for the Eugene McCarthy campaign in South Bend, Indiana. I worked out of a small office on Mishawaka Avenue in River Park. Either the McCarthy campaign in Indiana was poorly organized and they forgot about my office, or they decided they were unlikely to get very many votes in my blue collar neighborhood. Once they gave me a key, I never saw any one else from the campaign.

Occasionally I would find a box of new campaign literature sitting outside the door, but that was my only contact with the larger political world. No one from the neighborhood ever came in. Once I called up the city headquarters in downtown South Bend and volunteered to stuff mailboxes with the campaign pamphlets that were gathering dust in my little office, but they told me I should never go out on the street.

There was a coffee pot in the back room. I learned to make coffee, and then I learned to drink it. And in that back room I learned to smoke. I would sit on the unopened boxes of campaign brochures, drinking coffee and taking deep drags on my Taryton ("I'd rather fight than switch"), until my stomach churned and my head was swirling. I felt very lonely and very old.

Most of us who worked for McCarthy were bitter when Robert Kennedy joined the race. We felt he had waited until our man proved that hatred of the war could drive Johnson from office, and then Kennedy decided to come in on McCarthy's right. Despite our bitterness, everyone understood that Kennedy would probably win, and we became quietly wistful.

Kennedy came through South Bend once during the primary campaign. I joined the thousands of people who packed Notre Dame's Stepan Center to hear him. My corduroy jacket was covered with pins: No War, Clean for Gene, the stylized Picasso dove, and the chicken-foot peace sign. I thought I might have some kind of confrontation with the Kennedy supporters, but they ignored me. I don't remember anything the Senator said. There was lots of laughter. And wild cheering. He never mentioned McCarthy.

Even while I was feeling bitter about Kennedy's appeal, I was laughing and cheering like everyone else. When he finished, I pushed back through the crowd, ran across the parking lot, and stood by the only road his motorcade could take. No one else was there. After half an hour or so, I could see the cars moving slowly through the crowd in front of Stepan Center. A couple of police cars led a white convertible. Held tightly by their security people, Bobby and Ethel sat on the back of it, shaking hands with the young people who ran behind.

When they drove past me, I wanted to be part of it all, too. I ran as fast as I could. Everyone who had been following was out of breath, and I was suddenly alone with the Kennedys. I reached up and shook hands with Ethel, then Bobby. They were windblown, just like in their photographs, but they looked very tired. Their smiles were forced, almost unreal. Bobby's eyes were glazed. In this quick moment while I ran behind him, I thought he looked uncomfortable. Or maybe he looked sad. At the time I thought he looked like that because a kid covered in peace buttons was chasing him down a Midwestern street. I realized later that he hadn't really noticed.

"Good luck, Senator," I called out. He nodded and his staff pulled him into the car. They quickly accelerated and left me behind.

BANFF: RUNNING AWAY: DUCKS

If it happened now, I would know what the ducks were and might make a reasonable guess about why they had stayed so long into winter, swimming in the one bit of open water a couple of hundred yards above Bow Falls. The river's fast and noisy there, even when its surface is frozen.

> Two brown ducks, small, round, drifting down
> until blocked by ice, then climbing out
> to fly back to the top of open water.

The current pushes them downstream again
until one slips under. It never comes up.

It was the first day warm enough to wear sandals to the bar, and people seemed to be itching for a fight. A big oil-rig worker made a pass at Ted's wife, and she started yelling at him. I was trying to make peace when Ted exploded. He jumped right over me to hit the oil-rig guy square on the jaw. The guy didn't flinch. In fact, he sort of smiled. I made a dramatic show of pulling Ted away and knocked over all the bar stools in the process. One of them caught the nail on my big toe and ripped it off.

We hustled Ted out, almost threw him into his van, and told him to lie on the floor so the oil-rig guy couldn't see him if he decided to come looking. After I slammed the back door shut and was just beginning to worry about my bleeding toe, Ted's wife came around the side of the van and kissed me.

I was never really that kind of guy. I wanted to be a player, but I was never any good at it. And I never made passes at my friends' wives.

But that was not just a good-night peck. It was the real thing. I think there were tongues involved. She was still young, but a bit matronly, and she had long black hair. We'd been drinking and smoking for several hours, so I was surprised that her mouth felt cool. Clean. Certainly the best thing in my world that night.

And then she got in the van and drove off with her husband. I don't remember ever seeing her again. She and Ted already had three or four kids, but I heard they divorced shortly after. I ran into Ted once in a bar in Detroit and we drank for a while. I was embarrassed when he started throwing peanuts at a table of young women. They seemed to think it was funny, but I left. I didn't ask about his ex-wife.

JOHN GLENN HIGH SCHOOL, WESTLAND, MICHIGAN

homage to Mike Kelley

My first gig as visiting writer –
and they were excited too. Someone
made blue flyers for the doors and windows –
The poet is coming! The poet is
coming! The day I arrived someone
else had tagged every one of them –
in your mouth
in your mouth
in your mouth

PLOVERS AT THE MOUTH OF THE PLATTE

After a very hot day in early August, I went up from the cottage I was renting to the mouth of the Platte River at the south end of Sleeping Bear Dunes National Lakeshore. Mostly, I just wanted to cool off, to find a place on the edge of Lake Michigan where I could simply sit in the water and watch the sun set. But I also hoped that I might get a glimpse of one of the piping plovers that breed there.

The plovers are protected because they have almost died out along the Great Lakes. They have the bad fortune of making their shallow, exposed nests in the rocks and pebbles next to large sandy beaches, where we also like to hang out for much of the summer, playing games, walking our dogs, generally sinking into the glorious oblivion of summer by the lake. There might not be room for both of us. During much of the early summer, scientists—at least a few of them who think that perhaps we can coexist—build exclusion pens around the plover nests, and volunteers regularly monitor each one. Signs along the beach-front try to educate all of us about the birds and about the efforts to save them.

I didn't expect to find any piping plovers. These birds begin their migrations earlier than others, and have usually left by August or have gathered into flocks that pick bugs from the shoreline in more isolated sections of beach. Mostly I just wanted to cool off.

From the parking lot, I walked past the signs about the plovers, down along the bank of the Platte, where it cuts through the dunes in its last stretch before it arrives at the big lake. Even though the sun was setting into its August haze, it was still hot, probably somewhere in the low 90s, and the river was crowded with children drifting in the current. Near the mouth of the river, I crossed it, wading up to my waste in the cold water. I was already feeling better. The sun was setting and I was surrounded by that glow that seems to exist only on the Great Lakes during summer evenings. Two boys, who may have escaped straight from a Norman Rockwell painting, were skipping stones out into the water.

I walked past them, heading south along the shore, glancing down occasionally in the vague hope that I might find a Petoskey stone, or lifting my binoculars to look at a bird fly by. I had seen a couple of killdeer way down the beach, and I had tried to make them into the rare and endangered piping plovers. But they were too large, and they had double lines on their chests. They didn't have the bright orange legs I had seen in the bird books. I walked in the water, kicking along the gentle break of the waves, cooling off with every step.

I hadn't gone a hundred yards past the boys, when I noticed a shorebird flying toward me. I got my binoculars on it and saw that it had a very light back and a white rump. I thought I remembered that mark from the field books. I watched it fly by and up the shoreline, until it landed on the beach among a small group of five other birds that must have flown in behind me. I could see their dark eyes, their legs literally glowing orange in the light of the setting sun, and their small bright bills.

I caught my breath. There were probably less than 200 piping plovers on the coastlines of all the Great Lakes, and now six of them were right in front of me. I didn't move, but tried to steady my binoculars so I could get a good look at them.

And at that very moment the two cute little boys out doing their Huck Finn thing on a hot summer evening . . . threw stones at the plovers.

The birds fluttered up and away, none of them hurt. They flew out over the water, circled, and came back into the shore, clearly not overly frightened by the boys or their stones. I wanted to yell and wave my arms, but I was speechless. I started trudging toward the boys as quickly as I could.

Perhaps they had seen me watching the birds. Perhaps they were just a bit frightened by the sight of a sweaty Santa Claus coming straight for them through the sand. They turned up the beach and ran off, almost leaping through the river and back toward the parking lot. I saw that they talked to a man and a woman as they ran past.

I am not a person given to forcing his political views—even his environmental views—on strangers. Maybe I'll try to write about issues, or more likely simply try to describe things I find beautiful, but I never brow-beat strangers. Still, I walked straight up to this couple and greeted them.

"Those birds, the ones the boys were throwing stones at, they are the ones on the sign. The plovers. The protected endangered species." I let it all rush out, and tried to sound informative rather than judgmental.

"Oh, they shouldn't be throwing stones!" the woman said. "We'll talk to them about that." Clearly these people weren't going to be defensive or belligerent about the whole affair. My resolve was weakening.

"Boys have to throw stones," I said. "That's OK. Just not at these birds." And the three of us smiled and nodded our heads. I started to head back for my car, but I felt the need to say something more. To make more of a point. Perhaps to preach a bit. "These birds are just too precious," I turned and added. "Too beautiful."

Now the man and woman looked at me a bit indulgently, clearly trying to humor the crazy old guy out on the beach who was worried about birds. I felt I had to say even more to convince them about the seriousness of it all.

"And if they'd killed one—God forbid—well, it would have been a $250,000 fine." Now they looked a bit impressed. And they were suddenly looking at me as if I weren't quite so harmless.

I turned and kept walking.

BHARATPUR: DYING ANTELOPE

The nilgai   blue bull
close enough to cow
mother of us all
to be holy

is dying in a copse beside the road to the ecotourist lodge. No one dares euthanize it. Every morning the jackals and striped hyenas have moved closer, but they, too, seem governed by the prohibitions and wait for the nilgai to die.

At night their hungry howls
like surprised cries
from children in pain
startle our windows.

BIRD RESCUE

for Sherri Smith

Some reasonable people think
the horned grebe floating
down the Detroit River
between car-sized ice flows –
diving deep into current
to search for fish,
then rising into a pool
of oil or synthetic fuel –
deserved to die: maladjusted,
they say, to our new world.
But the grebe gasped its way
to shore-ice, water
seeping through spoiled feathers.

A sentimental soul found
it there, quivering in snow,
tried to wipe away the oil,
then brought it here. We warmed
the bird, fed it mealy worms
and waited for some liveliness
before bringing out our Dawn,
detergent of choice for bird rescue.

I stared into its red eye
and held the grebe, trembling
and tense, under a gentle stream
of water warmer than anything
it had felt in months,
while the real bird rescuer

worked the soap in, lifting
the oil out – she succeeded
when the feathers fluffed
on their own. The grebe was light
in my hands. Its hollow bones
felt delicate, breakable,
until a wing flapped against me,
strong and longing for flight.

A day later we took
our horned grebe down
to the Huron and the one patch
of open water below Barton Dam.
It scuttled out of its cage,
dove quickly, then surfaced
a few yards further away,
ruffled its feathers and drifted
down to join the indifferent ducks.

Soon enough, we hope,
it will run across water,
lift over ice, head north
perhaps, where it might find
its new and perfect life.

NO ONE DARED CALL IT BEAUTIFUL

(the Duck Lake Fire)

1.

No one died
but we paddled
quietly through the burn.
We avoided the snags, charred
even in mid-stream. Tag alders
and sedges already sprouted on the banks.

Some slopes and dune edges
were nothing but ash. They fluffed
away when we landed.
They crackled underfoot.

2.

Summer homes and businesses lost
in a May fire, then salvage logging
takes the larger dead trees for pulpwood.
Still, only a month later, I walk
through green patches of fresh bracken fern
under the black sticks that were jack pines.
Millions of cones, exploded open
and seedless, float down the Two Hearted.

ARGUMENT WITH EMILY: AMBER AFTERNOONS

Sunlight in the back room –
winter afternoons –
slants into corners
otherwise shaded –

the dark weeks – solstice
sun falling early –
low all day
across the yard –

but the back room –
these amber afternoons –
riots in its yellow light.

WINTER FINCHES

Christine chooses not to cut back
the stalks of our coneflowers
until spring, so the finches can pull
apart seeds all winter long.
They don't seem to appreciate that,
or the millet and thistle seeds,
the sunflower hearts and shelled peanuts
we buy for them. The gratitude's ours
when they descend every other day,
forty or fifty strong, a flurry
of light around the feeders.

. . .
just for a few weeks, from full summer
into September, on quiet days,
warm, humid but not hot—and the light
above the river turns green, like leaves,
reeds, water weeds or water itself
on its gently inexorable
slide through hills to the blue lakes beyond.

THE ALLEN CREEK DRAIN

for Margaret Wong

Somewhere under us a creek
finds its way to its river
and that river somehow finds
its way to the sea.

Somewhere under us flows the stream
we buried years ago,
once feared, now unremembered,
unbidden and necessary.

Somewhere under us the water
that once flooded a green meadow
oozes through the mud we've given it,
downward to its drain.

Somewhere under us a liquid grace
trying to find its way up
branches into channels like blood
in the arteries of our arms.

Somewhere under us is a choice
between fear and joy,
between the water we are
and the water we ignore.

Somewhere under us a creek
finds its green way
between strolling citizens of the city
we have dreamed.

Acknowledgments

Some of this work first appeared in *The Academy of American Poets poem-a-day* online site, *The Bear River Review*, *Border Crossing*, *Escape into Life* (online), *Fiddlehead* (Canada), *Hanging Loose*, *Hobart* (online), *Michigan Quarterly Review*, *Midwestern Gothic*, *Structo* (U.K.), and *Talking River*.

"Drummond Island Fossils" first appeared in *The Way North: Collected Upper Peninsula New Works*, edited by Ron Riekki (Wayne State University Press, 2013).

"Green Light" appeared in the chapbook *Marginalia for a Natural History* (Black Lawrence Press, 2011).

In "The Allen Creek Drain" the phrase "liquid grace" was borrowed, with permission, from Veronica Sanitate.

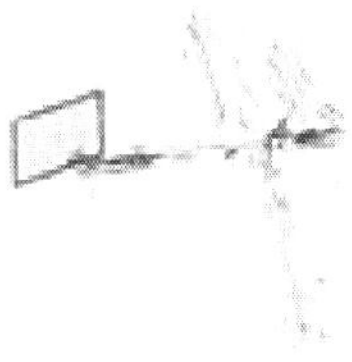

About the Author

KEITH TAYLOR has published fourteen earlier collections of poems and short stories, co-edited, or co-translated volumes. His work has appeared widely in journals, magazines, online sites, and newspapers in North America and Europe, as well as in many anthologies. He has received Fellowships from the National Endowment for the Arts and the Michigan Council for the Arts and Cultural Aff airs. He teaches at the University of Michigan, where he directs the Bear River Writers' Conference and works as Associate Editor of *Michigan Quarterly Review*. His website is www.keithtaylorannarbor.com.